THE NEW DESIGN

functional interiors

interiores funcionales

intérieurs fonctionnels

funktionale innenräume

Authors
Fernando de Haro & Omar Fuentes

Editorial Design & Production

Project Managers
Carlos Herver Díaz | Ana Teresa Vázquez de la Mora | Laura Mijares Castellá

Coordination
Ana Lydia Arcelus Cano | Cristina Gutiérrez Herce | Alejandra Martínez-Báez Aldama

Prepress Coordination
José Luis de la Rosa Meléndez

Copywriter
Víctor Hugo Martínez

English translation
Fionn Petch

French translation
Isadora Mora

German translation
Claudia Wondratschke

THE NEW DESIGN
FUNCTIONAL INTERIORS • INTERIORES FUNCIONALES • INTÉRIEURS FONCTIONNELS •
FUNKTIONALE INNENRÄUME

© 2013, Fernando de Haro & Omar Fuentes
AM Editores S.A. de C.V.
Paseo de Tamarindos 400 B, Suite 109, Col. Bosques de las Lomas, C.P. 05120, México D.F.
Tel. & Fax 52 (55) 5258 0279
ame@ameditores.com   www.ameditores.com

ISBN 978-607-437-275-5

Printed in China.

INDEX | ÍNDICE

INTRODUCTION
INTRODUCCIÓN
INTRODUCTION
EINLEITUNG

John Pawson, who is seen as the father of architectural minimalism, has defined this movement as the process of perfecting an artifact or space that has reached the limit of its possible reduction. It describes the quality of an atmosphere when each component, each detail, and each intersection has been condensed and reduced to its essence.

Functionalism in interior design and decoration shares this same objective of returning to the starting point of architecture's very nature, where nothing superficial or ornamental belongs to the scene, where function is to the fore and each space becomes as efficient as it is comfortable, without disregarding beauty. As a result, it is evident that the qualities of elegance and sobriety are favored when designing from the perspective described. These are not the only attributes: the blend of shapes, colors and elements is intended to provoke our senses while maintaining a balance in order to avoid negative excesses: neither nakedness, nor exuberance.

Given the above, it should be understood that functionalism is not a total denial of decoration, but on the contrary, its highly characteristic language permits surprising results when light, volume, geometry and an abundance of space emerge as the foremost decorative elements in the creative process.

This characteristic favors a clear and striking perception of architectural space, whether interiors or exteriors. The essential situation for achieving it is to ensure there are no superfluous elements that distract from the image produced, as in most cases this guarantees that a space becomes something worthy of contemplation. For this reason, if decorative pieces are used, these should function as seductive and warm visual accents that boost our perception of the whole, or subtly balance the resulting sobriety, which should never be cold or impersonal. Diaphanous spaces bathed in light, sequences of planes or walls in light colors, cladding in stone or wood: these are just a few of the basic elements that can be employed without restriction in both the public and private areas of our home.

Integration can be the most significant challenge of functionalism, even though as it has evolved over time it permits more colors, more details, and more decorative elements, with frankly surprising results. However, although the style has broadened, there is one thing it has jealously preserved: harmony. Nothing can undermine it, since it is the most highly-prized quality of interior architecture.

John Pawson, quien es considerado el padre del minimalismo arquitectónico, ha definido a este movimiento como el proceso de perfeccionar un artefacto o un espacio que ha llegado al límite de su reducción.

El funcionalismo en el diseño y la decoración interior tiene en común ese objetivo, volver al punto inicial de la naturaleza arquitectónica donde nada superficial u ornamental sea parte de la escena, donde la función sea perceptible y todo espacio se convierta tan eficaz como confortable sin menosprecio de la belleza. De ahí, lo evidente que resulta el hecho de que la elegancia y la sobriedad, sean atributos exaltados cuando se diseña. No son los únicos, la mezcla de formas, colores y elementos siempre favorece para provocar nuestros sentidos vigilando el equilibrio para no caer en excesos negativos: ni desnudez ni exuberancia.

Por lo anterior, debe considerarse, que el funcionalismo no es una negación absoluta a la decoración, por el contrario, su lenguaje –muy característico– permite resultados sorprendentes cuando en el proceso creativo, la luz, los volúmenes, el lenguaje geométrico, la amplitud espacial resultan ser los elementos decorativos prioritarios.

Esta característica favorece una percepción clara y contundente de los espacios arquitectónicos ya sea en interiores o exteriores, la si-tuación fundamental para lograrlo es cuidar que no existan elementos superfluos que enturbien la imagen que producen, pues así se logra en la mayoría de los casos que un espacio se convierta también en un objeto digno de contemplación. Por esta razón, si se emplean piezas decorativas, éstas deben funcionar como acentos visuales, seductores y cálidos que favorezcan nuestra percepción total del mismo o equilibren sutilmente la sobriedad resultante que nunca debe ser fría e impersonal. Los ambientes diáfanos colmados de luz, secuencias de planos o muros en colores claros, recubrimientos pétreos o maderas, son algunos de los elementos básicos, mismos que puede ser empleados sin restricción tanto en zonas públicas de nuestro hogar como en zonas privadas.

Unificar puede ser el reto más importante que el funcionalismo demande, debido a su evolución en el tiempo se ha permitido que hoy en día se integren más colores, más detalles, más elementos decorativos con resultados francamente sorprendentes; sin embargo, dentro de esa expansión del propio estilo, algo se ha conservado celosamente: la armonía. Nada puede atentar contra ella, es el valor más preciado para el ambiente y la arquitectura interior.

John Pawson, considéré le père du minimalisme dans l'architecture, défini ce mouvement comme «le processus d'optimisation d'un outil ou d'un espace qui ne peut plus être réduit au stricte minimum». Le minimalisme, c'est la capacité d'une atmosphère à condenser éléments, détails et intersections et à les réduire à son essence.

Le design et l'architecture d'intérieur ont un même objectif : retour à la caisse de départ de la nature architecturale où aucun détail —ni superficiel ni décoratif— fait partie du décor. La fonction y est perceptible et tout espace est aussi efficace que confortable, sans sous-estimer la beauté. L'élégance et la sobriété jouent un rôle important pour le type de design qui prend en compte ces principes. Mais il y en a d'autres principes : il faut favoriser le mélange de formes, couleurs et éléments pour exciter les sens tout, en conservant l'équilibre et éviter les excès. Il ne faut ni nudité ni exubérance.

Le fonctionnalisme n'est pas une négation absolue de la décoration. Au contraire, son langage —très singulier— produit des résultats impressionnants lorsque la lumière, le volume, le langage géométrique, l'amplitude spatiale sont les éléments décoratifs prioritaires.

Cette caractéristique favorise une perception claire et percutante des espaces architecturaux, intérieurs ou extérieurs. Or, la condition préalable pour y arriver est d'éliminer tout élément superflu qui vienne ternir une image digne d'un regard. Les objets décoratifs doivent être les marques visuelles séduisantes et chaleureuses qui favorisent une vue de l'ensemble ou qui équilibrent subtilement la sobriété en résultante, qui ne doit jamais être glaciale ou impersonnelle.

Des atmosphères diaphanes et lumineuses, des séquences de plans ou murs en couleurs claires, la pierre ou le bois en recouvrement, sont certains éléments de base que nous pouvons utiliser à cœur joie, que ce soit dans les pièces communes comme dans celles plus intimes.

Néanmoins, l'unification reste le plus grand défi à relever car, des nos jours, il est possible d'utiliser une palette de couleurs beaucoup plus complète et beaucoup plus de détails et d'objets décoratifs.

Le résultat est franchement surprenant. Dans toute cette évolution il ne reste qu'une seule à respecter : l'harmonie. Rien ne peut aller à son encontre car c'est l'élément le plus prisé pour l'architecture d'intérieur.

John Pawson, der Vater des architektonischen Minimalismus, hat diese Bewegung als den Prozess der Vervollkommnung eines Artefakts oder eines Raumes definiert, der an die Grenzen seiner Reduktion gekommen ist. Wo jede Komponente, jedes Detail, jede Raumtrennung verdichtet und auf das Wesentliche reduziert wird.

Der Funktionalismus im Design teilt dieses Ziel, indem er zurück zum Ausgangspunkt der architektonischen Natur geht, wo es nichts oberflächliches und auch keine Verzierungen gibt, wo jeder Raum genauso effizient wie auch komfortabel ist, ohne dabei die Schönheit zu vernachlässigen. Eleganz und Schlichtheit sind daher außerordentlich wichtige Attribute bei der Gestaltung. Die Mischung aus Formen, Farben und Elementen reizen unsere Sinne und wahren gleichzeitig das Gleichgewicht, um nicht in negative Exzesse zu verfallen: keine Nacktheit aber auch kein Überschwang.

Der Funktionalismus kommt dabei keiner absoluten Verweigerung der Dekoration gleich. Im Gegenteil ermöglicht seine -sehr charakteristische- Sprache überraschende Ergebnisse, wenn während des kreativen Prozesses das Licht, das Volumen, die geometrische Sprache und die Weite die vorrangigen dekorativen Elemente sind.

Es sollten keine überflüssigen Elemente das Gesamtbild trüben, denn in den meisten Fällen wird damit erreicht, dass ein Raum selbst zum Objekt der Betrachtung wird. Dekorative Elemente sollten wie visuelle, verführerische und warme Akzente eingesetzt werden oder einen subtilen Ausgleich zu der daraus resultierenden Nüchternheit, die niemals kalt und unpersönlich sein darf, schaffen.

Die luftigen hellen Zimmer, Ebenen oder Wände in hellen Farben, Verkleidungen aus Stein oder Holz sind einige der Grundelemente, die ohne Einschränkungen sowohl in den öffentlichen Räumen eines Hauses, als auch im privaten Bereich eingesetzt werden können.

Die Vereinheitlichung ist vielleicht die wichtigste Herausforderung, nach der der Funktionalismus verlangt. Innerhalb seiner Entwicklung wurde mit der Zeit gestattet, dass heute mehr Farben, mehr Details, mehr dekorative Elemente integriert werden dürfen mit geradezu erstaunlichen Ergebnissen. Dennoch ist in dieser Erweiterung des ihm eigenen Stils etwas erhalten geblieben, die Harmonie. Nichts kann sie bedrohen, sie ist der kostbarste Schatz der Umwelt und der Innenarchitektur.

BEDROOMS

DORMITORIOS

CHAMBRES À COUCHER

SCHLAFZIMMER

A bedroom is our most intimate refuge and one that offers us a place of rest. Its functionality lies in its specific capacity to satisfy this purpose. To achieve this in a harmonious manner, items of furniture may be used for different functions, including the possibility of acting as decorative elements.

Un dormitorio es el refugio más íntimo que garantiza nuestro descanso, en él, la funcionalidad radica en que éste satisfaga estrictamente esa premisa. Para lograrlo con armonía, los muebles pueden ser utilizados cumpliendo diferentes funciones incluyendo la posibilidad de actuar como elementos decorativos.

Une chambre est le refuge le plus intime pour y trouver le repos, la fonction principale de cette pièce. Pour aboutir à cet objectif, les meubles peuvent remplir plusieurs fonctions, même celle de décorer.

Ein Schlafzimmer ist der intimste Rückzugsort, der unsere Ruhe garantieren sollte, ihm inhärent ist demnach die Funktionalität, damit er diese Voraussetzung streng erfüllt. Um Harmonie herzustellen, können die Möbel verschiedene Funktionen erfüllen, einschließlich der Möglichkeit als dekorative Elemente zu fungieren.

This bedroom has the virtue of maximizing its space which together with the refined design of the furniture means that all the compositional elements are displayed with total elegance. Thus there is the bed with its designer lines and multi-functionality; the diaphanous colors of an unadorned architecture and small constructional details that subtly match, generating a harmony ideal for rest.

Este dormitorio tiene la gran cualidad de maximizar la amplitud del espacio y en conjunto con el diseño refinado del mobiliario provoca que todos los elementos compositivos se perciban con absoluta elegancia. Así, es la cama con sus líneas de diseño y su multifuncionalidad; los colores diáfanos de una arquitectura sin ornamento y pequeños detalles constructivos los que se corresponden con sutileza generando una armonía idónea para el descanso.

Cette chambre optimise l'espace, grâce au design raffiné du mobilier, tous les autres éléments qui la composent acquièrent cette même élégance. Le design et les multiples fonctions du lit ; une architecture sans éléments décoratifs et aux couleurs claires, avec juste quelques détails dans la construction, dotent cette chambre d'une harmonie idéale pour le repos.

Dieses Schlafzimmer verfügt über die große Eigenschaft, zum einen die Weite des Raumes zu maximieren und zum anderen mit einem raffinierten Möbeldesign zu bewirken, dass alle Kompositionselemente mit absoluter Eleganz wahrgenommen werden. So wie das Bett mit seinem Design und seiner Multifunktionalität; die transparenten Farben einer schnörkellosen Architektur und kleine Konstruktionsdetails, die auf subtile Weise eine perfekte Harmonie schaffen, die zum entspannen einlädt.

multifunctional design

diseño multifuncional

les multiples fonctions du design

multifunktionales design

Multi-functionality in furniture design is one of the principal characteristics of avant-garde and contemporary style: in this case, the dual function of the furniture meets a range of needs.

La multifuncionalidad del diseño del mobiliario es una de las características principales de la vanguardia y el estilo contemporáneo: en este caso, la doble función del mobiliario satisface diversas necesidades.

L'avant-gardisme et le style contemporain se caractérisent para la multiple fonctionnalité de son mobilier : un objet devient d'autant plus relevant aux yeux de l'utilisateur que lorsqu'l satisfait plusieurs besoins.

Das multifunktionale Design der Möbel ist eine der Haupteigenschaften der Avantgarde und des zeitgenössischen Stils. In diesem Fall erfüllt die Doppelfunktion der Möbel verschiedene Bedürfnisse.

Each detail of design in the
furniture opens up the possibility of highlighting the degree
of functionalism we intend to
achieve with our spaces.

Cada detalle diseñado en el
mobiliario nos abre la posibilidad de enfatizar el grado de
funcionalismo que pretendemos
alcanzar en nuestros espacios.

Chacun des détails qui dessine
le mobilier est une possibilité
de souligner le fonctionnalisme
que nous souhaitons avoir dans
nos espaces.

Jedes Detail des Möbeldesigns
eröffnet uns die Möglichkeit,
den Grad des Funktionalismus
zu betonen, den wir in unseren
Räumen erreichen wollen.

storage

guardado

rangement

aufbewahrung

The color white is one of the most frequently used, since it makes it possible to maintain a clean visual space, enhancing the characteristics of the furniture without ignoring harmony.

El color blanco es uno de lo más socorridos porque permite mantener una limpieza visual en el espacio, realzando las características del mobiliario sin menosprecio de la armonía.

L'on revient souvent au blanc car cette couleur nous permet d'offrir une vue dégagée de l'espace. Le blanc nous permet de souligner les caractéristiques du mobilier sans sous-estimer l'harmonie.

Weiß ist eine der bewährtesten Farben, weil sie im Raum eine visuelle Reinheit erzeugt und die Eigenschaften des Mobiliars hervorhebt, ohne dabei die Harmonie zu stören.

Focusing on the play of light and shadow allows us to take away ornamental objects, resulting in a serene ambiance with a welcoming aspect.

Privilegiando al juego de luz y sombras puede prescindirse de objetos ornamentales obteniendo un ambiente sereno con una estética muy acogedora.

Avec un jeu d'ombres et de lumières nous pouvons nous passer d'objets décoratifs et nous aurons comme résultat une décoration sereine et très chaleureuse.

Verwendet man das Spiel von Licht und Schatten als gestalterisches Element, kann man auf Dekorationsgegenstände verzichten und erzielt ein ruhiges, gemütliches Ambiente.

optimizing spaces

optimización del espacio

optimiser l'espace

optimierung der räume

Thanks to the creativity and geometric design of pure lines, furnishings can reveal functional spaces that integrate ornamental objects at different scales.

Gracias a la creatividad y el diseño geométrico de líneas puras, el mobiliario puede revelar espacios funcionales integrando objetos ornamentales de diferentes escalas.

Grâce à la créativité et au design géométrique des lignes épurées, le mobilier peut dévoiler des espaces fonctionnels et y ajouter des objets décoratifs de différentes tailles.

Dank der Kreativität und des geometrischen Designs basierend auf klaren Linien, kann man mit der Inneneinrichtung funktionale Räume schaffen, in die man dann Dekorationsgegenstände verschiedener Größe integriert.

The natural beauty of wood or vegetation can become the main decorative feature of a bedroom, making it a warmer or fresher space as desired.

La belleza natural de la madera o la vegetación, pueden convertirse en los principales atributos decorativos de un dormitorio haciéndolo más cálido o fresco según se desee.

Le bois et la végétation ont une beauté naturelle qui peut devenir l'atout essentiel dans la décoration d'une chambre. Elle peut être fraîche ou chaleureuse, selon les souhaits.

Holz oder Pflanzen haben eine natürliche Schönheit. Sie können zu den wesentlichen dekorativen Attributen eines Schlafzimmers werden, das sie, je nach Wunsch, entweder wärmer oder frischer erscheinen lassen.

The selection and arrangement of the furniture is an important factor for creating a practical space in line with the purpose of the room and the needs of the person who occupies it.

El acomodo de los muebles y la selección de los mismos es un factor importante para poder lograr un espacio práctico de acuerdo con la función del cuarto y las necesidades de quien lo va a vivir.

Le choix des meubles et sa disposition dans une pièce nous permettra d'aménager un espace pratique, à même de répondre aux besoins de l'habitant.

Die Auswahl und Anordnung der Möbel sind wichtig, um einen Raum gemäß seiner Funktion und den Bedürfnissen der Person, die darin lebt, praktisch zu gestalten.

BATHROOMS

BAÑOS
SALLES DE BAINS
BÄDER

A good bathroom, as well as functional, should be a space of exceptional comfort. It is one of the refuges where design is placed at the service of the body. This means that the circulations, the visual cleanliness, the finishes or construction details, together with the furnishing, lighting and service areas, form a group of elements that enable us to feel fulfilled.

Un buen baño, además de funcional, debe de ser un espacio de comodidad extrema. Se trata de uno de los refugios donde el diseño debe consentir a nuestro cuerpo. De ahí que las circulaciones, la pulcritud visual, los remates o detalles constructivos sean en conjunto con el mobiliario, la iluminación y las zonas de servicio o de apoyo, un conjunto de factores que nos hagan sentir plenos.

Une bonne salle de bain est fonctionnelle est extrêmement confortable. Il s'agit d'un refuge ou la décoration doit être au service du bien-être corporel. La circulation, les finitions et la vue dégagée doivent accompagner le mobilier et l'éclairage afin de satisfaire pleinement nos besoins.

Ein gutes Badezimmer sollte funktional, aber auch extrem komfortabel sein. Das Bad ist ein Rückzugsort, dessen Design unseren Körper verwöhnen sollte. Daher sind die begehbaren Bereiche, visuelle Reinheit, Verzierungen oder Baudetails in Kombination mit den Möbeln, der Beleuchtung und den Servicebereichen Faktoren, die uns ein angenehmes Gefühl verleihen sollen.

The design of multifunctional furnishings allows us to emphasize the qualities of an intimate space like a bathroom. Without disregarding the comfort and ease of having everything within arm's reach, it is essential to achieve an efficient layout that allows us to move around and make use of all the spaces at our disposal. Ordering the space is a task to be resolved with elegance and sophistication, and one that also brings to the fore architectural design proposals emphasized by the treatment of ceilings, mirrors, the choice of blinds, decorative objects or vegetation.

El diseño de muebles multifuncionales nos permite destacar las cualidades de un espacio íntimo como lo es un baño. Sin menosprecio de la comodidad y la facilidad de tener todo a nuestro alcance, resulta clave lograr un acomodo eficiente que nos permita circular y hacer uso de todos los espacios que estén a nuestra disposición. Ordenar el espacio puede ser una tarea que se solucione con elegancia y sofisticación y que además haga lucir intenciones del diseño arquitectónico enfatizadas por el tratamiento en plafones, el diseño de espejos, la selección de persianas u objetos decorativos o vegetación.

Les meubles qui remplissent plusieurs fonctions nous permettent de mettre en avant les qualités d'une pièce aussi intime qu'une salle de bain. Sans sous-estimer le confort et l'aspect pratique d'avoir tout à portée de main, il faut concevoir un rangement efficace nous permettant de circuler facilement et de bien profiter de chacun des espaces disponibles. Nous pouvons aménager l'espace de manière à mettre en avant —avec élégance et sophistication— l'intention de la conception architecturale. Plafonds, glaces, persiennes, objets décoratifs et végétation sont à notre disposition pour atteindre cet objectif.

Das Design von Multifunktionsmöbeln ermöglicht es uns, die Eigenschaften eines intimen Raums wie ein Bad, hervorzuheben, ohne dabei den Komfort, und die Leichtigkeit alles in Reichweite zu haben, zu vernachlässigen. Dabei ist eine effiziente Ordnung entscheidend, die es uns ermöglicht uns frei zu bewegen und alle Bereiche zu nutzen, die uns zur Verfügung stehen. Die Organisation eines Raumes stellt eine Aufgabe dar, die mit Eleganz und Raffinesse gelöst werden kann. Außerdem wird durch die Gestaltung der Decke, das Design der Spiegel, die Auswahl von Jalousien oder durch dekorative Objekte und Pflanzen die architektonische Gestaltung betont.

innovative design
diseño innovador
conception innovante
innovatives design

Functionalist design means it is possible to innovate using only a few elements. In this case, striking features include the variation in lighting, the contrast between materials and forms, and the transparency of open elements and the solemnity of more intimate spaces.

El diseño funcionalista permite ser innovador con pocos elementos en juego, en este caso destacan las variaciones lumínicas, el contraste entre materiales y formas, así como la transparencia entre elementos abiertos y la solemnidad de espacios más íntimos.

Un design fonctionnel permet d'innover avec très peu d'éléments. Ici, nous jouons avec l'éclairage, le contraste de formes et des matériaux, la transparence des objets ouverts et la solennité des espaces intimes.

Das funktionalistische Design kann mit Hilfe weniger Elemente sehr innovativ wirken. Eine Rolle spielen in diesem Fall die Lichtverhältnisse, der Kontrast zwischen Materialien und Formen sowie die Transparenz zwischen offenen Elementen und die Erhabenheit intimer Räume.

Free of elements that might distract the gaze, objects reveal their visual essence, a specific refinement where precision and function are qualities to be praised.

Libres de elementos que puedan distraer la mirada, los objetos revelan su máxima estética, un refinamiento preciso donde la precisión y la función son cualidades enaltecidas.

Loin d'éléments qui font détourner le regard, les objets dévoilent leur plus grande beauté, une stylisation où la précision et la fonctionnalité sont mis en exergue.

Frei von Elementen, die das Auge des Betrachters ablenken können, offenbaren die Objekte ihre höchstmögliche Ästhetik, eine präzise Raffinesse, wo Präzision und Funktion edle Eigenschaften darstellen.

storage

guardado

rangement

aufbewahrung

Assigning areas exclusively to storage allows us to achieve a visual purity that is reflected in an atmosphere of comfort and cleanliness. This is an essential characteristic to emphasize the fusion of design and architectural elements.

Destinar zonas exclusivas para el guardado nos permitirá obtener una limpieza visual que se traducirá en una atmósfera de confort y pulcritud. Una característica esencial para lucir las cualidades del diseño y la arquitectura fusionadas.

Compter avec des espaces destinés au rangement nous permet d'offrir une vue dégagée de la pièce et de recréer une atmosphère propre et confortable. Condition sine qua non pour mettre en avant les attributs du design et de l'architecture.

Wenn gewisse Bereiche ausschließlich der Aufbewahrung von Dingen dienen, erhalten wir eine visuelle Ordnung, die durch eine Atmosphäre von Komfort und Sauberkeit unterstrichen wird. Eine wesentliche Eigenschaft, um die Qualitäten einer Verbindung von Design und Architektur hervorzuheben.

Blending elements and languages makes it possible to highlight in a striking manner an item of furniture or a space, above all when color is the principal feature.

Mezclar elementos y lenguajes permite que se destaque contundentemente un mueble o un espacio, sobre todo cuando el color es un añadido principal.

Le mélange d'éléments et langages nous permet de mettre en avant et de manière percutante un meuble ou un espace. Surtout si la couleur est l'élément ajouté.

Die Mischung von Elementen erlaubt es ein Möbelstück oder einen Raum nachdrücklich zu betonen, vor allem dann, wenn die Farbe einen wesentlichen Akzent setzt.

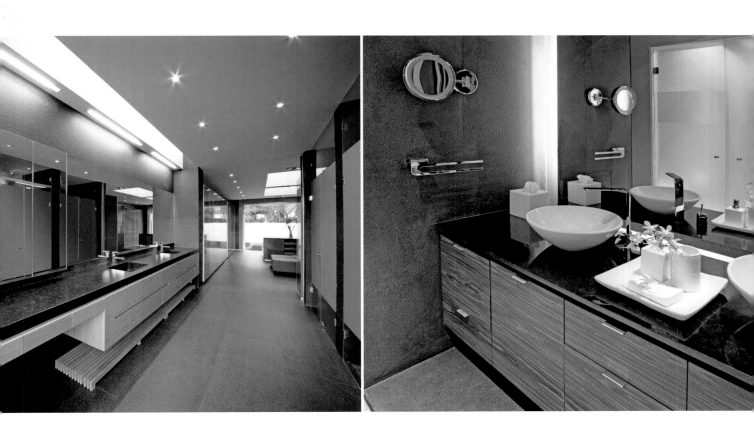

A few gestures can produce quality designs that are irresistible and visually powerful, with no need for further accessories or ornament to make sense.

Pocos gestos pueden producir diseños de calidad, irresistibles y visualmente poderosos, no necesitan ni accesorios ni ornamentos para cobrar sentido.

Avec très peu de gestes nous pouvons produire un design de qualité, irrésistible et attrayant, qui n'a pas besoin d'accessoires ou d'ornement pour prendre du sens.

Hochwertige, überzeugende und bildstarke Designs können schon anhand weniger Details erreicht werden und kommen ohne Accesoires oder Verzierungen aus.

optimizing spaces
optimización del espacio
optimiser l'espace
optimierung der räume

Everything is a part of everything else. Following this principal of unity, minimalist decoration requires that the functions of a space are imperceptible to the gaze. Silently maintained, beauty is found in the order and positioning of the objects.

Todo es parte de todo. Bajo este principio de unidad, la decoración minimalista exige que las funciones de un espacio sean imperceptibles a la mirada. Sigilosamente cuidada, la belleza recae en el orden y posición de los objetos.

Cela fait partie d'un tout. Sous le principe d'unité, la déco minimaliste exige que les fonctions d'un espace soient imperceptibles au regard. Discrètement soignés, l'ordre et la disposition des objets sont en charge de la beauté de l'espace.

Alles ist ein Teil von allem. Nach diesem Prinzip der Einheit erfordert die minimalistische Einrichtung, dass die Funktionen eines Raumes für das Auge fast unmerklich sind. Lautlos behütet liegt die Schönheit in der Anordnung und der Position von Objekten.

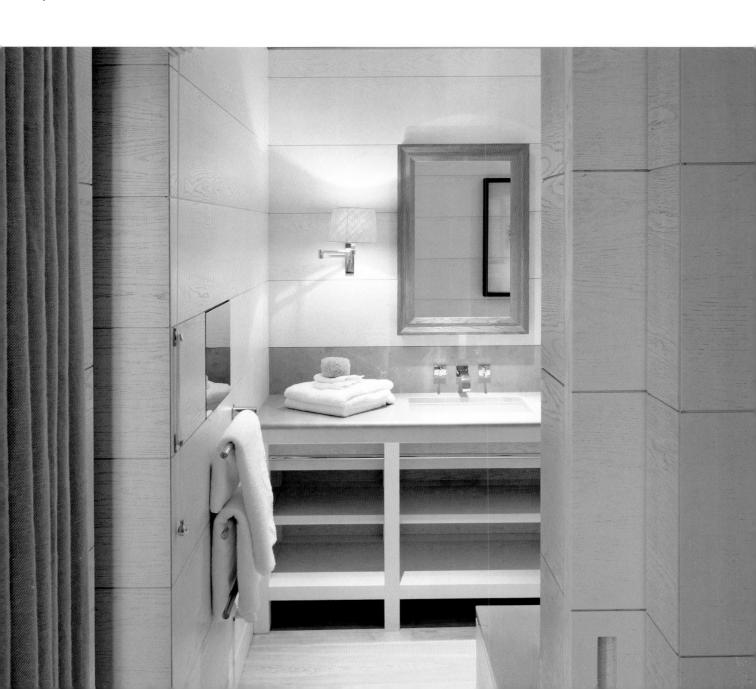

An ideal palette of materials for these spaces comprises two elements; including a third works well if we wish to emphasize it as a decorative gesture.

Una paleta de materiales idónea para estos ambientes se compone de dos elementos, incluir un tercero funciona bien para destacarlo como un gesto decorativo.

La gamme de matériaux idéal pour ces pièces n'a que deux éléments. Si vous en ajoutez un troisième, celui là fonctionnera comme objet décoratif.

Eine Materialpalette, die ideal für diese Umgebungen ist, besteht aus zwei Elementen. Wird ein drittes dazu genommen, kann dieses gut eine dekorative Funktion übernehmen.

Walnut wood contrasted with the smooth white color of the walls results in a solemn but warm finish. A similar effect is achieved when using stone in the manner of a grand visual canvas.

La madera de nogal contrastada con el color blanco de los muros sin textura, da como resultado un acabado solemne pero cálido. Algo similar sucede al incorporar piedra como un gran lienzo pictórico.

Pour une touche solennelle mais chaleureuse, utilisez le bois de noyer pour le contraster à un mur blanc sans texture. Vous obtenez un résultat similaire lorsque vous utilisez une pierre à la place d'un grand tableau.

Das Walnussholz kontrastiert mit dem Weiß der glatten Wände, das Resultat ist ein elegantes aber warmes Finish. Etwas Ähnliches geschieht, wenn man Stein wie eine große Bildleinwand verarbeitet.

KITCHENS & DINING ROOMS

COCINAS Y COMEDORES

CUISINES ET SALLES À MANGER

KÜCHEN UND ESSZIMMER

Without a doubt, the kitchen should be decorated with the fact that it is above all a functional space in mind. On this basis, its layout may be arranged based on the distribution of the space, its cleanliness, maintenance, and the forms and colors of the materials, appliances, or dining area. Recently, the focus has been on designing open-plan kitchens conceived as a meeting place for socializing or enjoying food, making for an experience.

Sin lugar a duda la cocina debe decorarse tomando en cuenta que es ante todo un espacio primordialmente funcional; partiendo de ahí, su configuración se puede jerarquizar basándose en la distribución del espacio, su limpieza, mantenimiento, las formas y los colores de los materiales, equipos o el comedor. Recientemente se enfatiza la cualidad de diseñar cocinas abiertas donde sea posible concebirlas como centro de reunión para socializar y degustar en ellas, toda una experiencia.

Lorsque l'on pense à décorer une cuisine, il faut que la fonctionnalité l'emporte sur tout le reste. Nous pouvons partir de ce principe pour ensuite prendre en compte la distribution de l'espace, la propreté, l'entretien, les formes et les couleurs des matériaux, l'équipement et la salle à manger. Il y a une tendance à concevoir des cuisines ouvertes qui deviennent le lieu de rencontre pour socialiser et déguster. C'est une expérience à part entière.

Zweifellos sollte die Küche mit dem Bewusstsein dekoriert werden, dass sie in erster Linie ein funktionaler Raum ist. Von dort ausgehend, kann ihre Gestaltung hierarchisch vorgenommen werden, basierend auf der Aufteilung des Raumes, seiner Reinigung, Pflege, der Formen und Farben der Materialien, der Ausstattung oder des Esstisches. Unlängst konzentriert man sich auf die Gestaltung offener Küchen, die als gesellschaftlicher Treffpunkt begriffen werden und gleichzeitig ein Erlebnisort sind, wo gute Speisen genossen werden können.

A kitchen may take on a more old-fashioned, warm appearance when it is based around dark wood with a prominent grain, which contrasts elegantly with colors like black or purple. On the other hand, if the aim is to create a more diaphanous and transparent effect, light shades may be used alongside bright colors such as yellow or white. The exacting choice of furniture and ornament is fundamental.

Una cocina puede tener una apariencia más rústica y cálida cuando se usan como recubrimientos base las maderas en tonalidades oscuras con vetas muy grandes que se pueden contrastar elegantemente con colores como el negro o el violeta. Por el contrario, si lo que se desea es generar una imagen más diáfana y transparente puede recurrirse a tonalidades claras y colores vivos como el amarillo o el blanco. La selección minuciosa de mobiliario y ornamento es fundamental.

Pour une cuisine rustique et chaleureuse, utilisez le bois veiné en couleurs foncés. Pour une touche d'élégance, contrastez-le avec le noir ou le violet. Si, au contraire, vous souhaitez une cuisine plus claire, utilisez les couleurs claires et contrastez-les avec des couleurs vives comme le jaune ou le blanc. Un choix soigné du mobilier et des objets décoratifs est de la plus haute importance.

Eine Küche kann ein rustikales und warmes Aussehen haben, wenn man als Verkleidung vor allem dunkle Holztöne mit sehr großen Maserungen benutzt, die elegant mit Farben wie Schwarz oder Violett kontrastiert werden können. Umgekehrt, wenn man ein klares und transparentes Erscheinungsbild erreichen möchte, kann man auf lebendige Farben wie gelb oder weiß zurückgreifen. Die sorgfältige Auswahl der Möbel und die Dekoration ist von grundlegender Bedeutung.

innovative design
diseño innovador
conception innovante
innovatives design

Canvases set against walls of Venetian glass tiles, combined with the chrome of the kitchen appliances, complement and play off each other in the presence of works of art in a contemporary kitchen.

Los lienzos en muros hechos con mosaicos venecianos, así como el cromo en los equipo de cocina conjugan y se complementan con audacia ante la presencia de obras de arte en una cocina contemporánea.

Une cuisine contemporaine permet de combiner avec audace : des murs lambrissés de carrelage vénitien, un équipement de cuisine en peinture chromé et des œuvres d'art.

Die Gemälde aus venezianischen Mosaiken an der Wand und das Chrom der Küchengeräte ergänzen sich und lassen sich in einer modernen Küche auch sehr gut mit Kunstwerken kombinieren.

An open-air kitchen is ideal for incorporating striking objects that balance the severity of the metallic elements, creating a pleasant space.

Una cocina al aire libre es idónea para incorporar objetos sumamente llamativos que equilibren la dureza de los elementos metálicos haciéndola muy placentera.

A une cuisine à l'extérieur, nous pouvons ajouter des objets attrayants pour contre-carrer la rigidité des éléments métalliques et la rendre plus accueillante.

Eine Küche unter freiem Himmel ist ideal, um sehr auffällige Objekte, die die Härte von Metallelementen auszugleichen vermögen, zu integrieren und damit eine angenehme Umgebung zu schaffen.

A contemporary kitchen has the quality of converting the food preparation area into a communal zone, where it is important that the furniture is comfortable and propitious for conversation.

Una cocina contemporánea tiene la cualidad de convertir la zona de preparación de alimentos en una zona de convivencia, es importante que el mobiliario que se emplee sea confortable y propicie la conversación.

Une cuisine contemporaine transforme une pièce vouée à la préparation de repas en un lieu d'échange. Il convient de choisir un mobilier confortable et compact pour que l'on y trouve suffisamment d'espace pour participer aux conversations

Eine moderne Küche hat die Eigenschaft, den Kochbereich gleichzeitig auch zu einem Bereich des Zusammenlebens zu machen. Die Möbel, die verwendet werden, sollten unbedingt komfortabel sein.

optimizing spaces

optimización del espacio

optimiser l'espace

optimierung der räume

One of the most effective ways of creating an efficient cooking area is to design a fitted kitchen where all the appliances are incorporated into the units, in order to suit the available space.

Una de las maneras más eficaces de hacer eficiente el espacio al cocinar es diseñar una cocina integral donde se alojen todos los equipos dentro del mobiliario diseñado a la medida del espacio arquitectónico.

Pour optimiser l'espace, choisissez une cuisine équipée, complètement adaptée à l'espace architectural, pour y ranger tous les éléments de cuisine.

Einer der effektivsten Wege, um eine Küche effizienter zu machen, ist das Design einer Einbauküche, wo die gesamte Ausstattung in das Mobiliar integriert wird, welches wiederrum den architektonischen Begebenheiten angepasst wird.

When the available space is limited, it is worth emphasizing a circulation area and incorporating decorative elements of small or medium size.

Cuando el espacio es reducido conviene enfatizar una zona de circulación e incorporar elementos decorativos de formato medio o pequeño.

Dans un espace étroit, mettez l'accent sur l'espace de circulation et ajoutez des objets décoratifs en petit ou moyen format.

Wenn wenig Platz ist, sollte ein begehbarer Bereich betont, und mittelgroße und kleine dekorative Elemente integriert werden.

A kitchen can also have a playful or fun aspect: all it needs is a functional object taken to an almost sculptural extreme, or a richly-colored visual finish.

Una cocina también puede tener una apariencia lúdica o divertida: basta un objeto funcional llevado casi escultórico o un remate visual muy colorido.

Une cuisine peut aussi être ludique : il suffit d'ajouter un objet fonctionnel, mis en valeur comme s'il s'agissait d'une sculpture. Ou bien, ajoutez un objet visuel très coloré.

Eine Küche kann auch spielerisch und heiter aussehen. Dafür reicht schon ein fast skulpturartiges funktionales Objekt oder ein sehr bunter Augenfang.

STUDIES & LOUNGES

ESTUDIOS Y SALAS DE ESTAR

BUREAUX ET SALLES DE SÉJOUR

WOHN - UND ARBEITSZIMMER

Including a subtle play of textures is of the greatest importance in areas for sharing or enjoying over long periods. This helps to ensure the gaze is always entertained, and does not become dulled to detail. Special attention must be paid to adding decorative objects that always maintain a visual composition and hierarchy; textures and scales may be combined but should not be scattered around in a haphazard manner. Order is fundamental.

Incluir un delicado juego de texturas es sumamente importante en espacios donde la convivencia y el tiempo para usarlos puedan ser prolongados. Con ello se favorece que nuestra mirada no caiga monótonamente y se debilite para perder atención por el detalle. Debe tenerse especial cuidado en agregar objetos decorativos que mantengan siempre una composición y una jerarquía visual, se pueden combinar texturas y escalas pero nunca ubicarlos de modo caprichoso. El orden es fundamental.

Pour ces pièces vouées à une convivialité prolongée, choisissez des textures délicates. Ainsi, notre regard ne sera pas hébété par l'attention qu'exigent les nombreux détails d'une pièce. Ajoutez des objets décoratifs qui vont respecter la composition et la hiérarchie visuelle. Vous pouvez combiner les tailles et les textures mais vous ne devez jamais les organiser de manière aléatoire. L'ordre est primordial.

In Räumen, wo man sich versammelt und sich länger aufhält, ist eine zarte Mischung an Strukturen extrem wichtig. Damit sorgt man dafür, dass der Blick nicht müde, und die Liebe zum Detail nicht gemindert werden. Man sollte vor allem darauf achten, dass wenn dekorative Objekte in den Raum integriert werden, deren Anordnung immer einer visuellen Hierarchie folgt. Texturen und unterschiedliche Größen können kombinieren werden, sollten aber nie willkürlich platziert werden. Die Anordnung ist sehr wichtig.

Although almost eclectic in style given the large number of decorative items and objects, with their various forms, textures and colors, something in this space serves to unite the diversity: the presence of neutral colors (white and gray) in the architecture, which serve as a backdrop against which objects stands out, without overloading the décor. Another element that works in its favor is the natural illumination of the space.

Casi al límite de llegar a un estilo ecléctico por la cantidad de piezas y objetos decorativos así como sus formas, texturas o colores, algo en este espacio armoniza la diversidad evidente: la presencia de colores neutros (blanco y gris) en la arquitectura, los cuales funcionan como fondo en el que se destaca cada objeto sin recargar negativamente la decoración. Sin duda otro elemento que juega a favor es la iluminación natural del espacio.

Voici une décoration au style quasi éclectique : objets décoratifs, formes, textures et couleurs. Quelque chose dans cette pièce rétablit l'harmonie : les couleurs neutres (blanc et gris) de l'architecture servent de toile de fond sur lequel chaque objet est mis en avant sans trop charger la décoration. Sans doute, la lumière naturelle y joue en rôle important.

Obwohl bedingt durch die Anzahl an Dekorationsobjekten, ihrer Formen, Texturen und Farben fast am Limit eines eklektischen Stils angekommen, harmonisiert etwas in diesem Raum diese offensichtliche Vielfalt: die neutralen Farben (weiß und grau) der Architektur, die als Hintergrund fungieren. Jedes Objekt wird durch sie, ohne die Einrichtung negativ zu beeinflussen, hervorgehoben. Ohne Zweifel hat auch ein weiteres Element positiven Einfluss, die natürliche Beleuchtung des Raumes.

optimizing spaces

optimización del espacio

optimiser l'espace

optimierung der räume

One way of optimizing space and decorating it in a single gesture is through the use of shelves integrated into niches. These should match the finishes of the floors or the textures of the furniture.

Una manera de optimizar el espacio y decorarlo en un solo gesto es a través de repisas integradas a nichos arquitectónicos. Éstas deben procurar mimetizarse con los acabados en pisos o las texturas de los muebles.

Installer des étagères encastrées aux niches est une excellente manière d'optimiser l'espace. Les étagères doivent se mimétiser avec les finitions des sols ou les textures des meubles.

Der Raum kann durch die Integration von Regalen in architektonischen Nischen optimiert und dekoriert werden. Dabei sollte man versuchen, diese mit den Bodenbelägen oder Texturen der Möbel abzustimmen.

Reusing antique furniture is ideal for adapting spaces and endowing them with personality and a vintage style. Light colors avoid over-saturation of the gaze, and offer a solution that provides a touch of elegance.

La reutilización de mobiliario antiguo puede ser idónea para acondicionar espacios dotándolos de personalidad y un estilo *vintage*, los colores claros permiten no recargar visualmente esta solución logrando además un toque de elegancia.

Récupérer un mobilier usé nous permet de réaménager des espaces, leur donnant un style retro et une personnalité. Les couleurs claires permettent d'offrir une vue dégagée et apportent une touche d'élégance.

Die Verwendung von antiken Möbeln ist ideal, um Räumen Persönlichkeit und einen gewissen Vintage-Stil zu geben. Helle Farben vermeiden eine visuelle Überfrachtung und verleihen einen Hauch von Eleganz.

The space created beneath a staircase can offer a superb corner for reading, and the unusual function means the bookcase becomes a decorative element.

El espacio que se genera debajo de la escalera puede ser un gran lugar para leer, adquiriendo una función inusual el librero se convierte en elemento decorativo.

Sous les escaliers nous pouvons aménager un coin lecture. Dans cette occasion unique, l'armoire à livres devient l'objet décoratif.

Der Raum unter einer Treppe eignet sich hervorragend dazu, um darunter zu lesen. Das Bücherregal erhält dadurch eine ungewöhnliche Funktion und verwandelt sich in ein dekoratives Element.

innovative design
diseño innovador
conception innovante
innovatives design

Light is the principal element for perceiving a dynamic space that is transformed over the day; the variety of tones and styles will serve to highlight an eclectic solution that suggests a highly avant-garde appearance.

La luz es el principal elemento para percibir un espacio dinámico que se transforma a lo largo del día, la variedad de tonos y estilos acentuará una solución ecléctica haciéndolo lucir altamente vanguardista.

L'éclairage est l'élément clé pour un espace qui se transforme tout au long de la journée. La nuance des couleurs et des styles donne comme résultat une décoration éclectique et avant-gardiste.

Licht ist das wichtigste Element, um einen Raum dynamisch zu gestalten. Dieser verwandelt sich im Laufe des Tages, die Vielzahl von Farben und Stile unterstreichen eine eklektische Lösung und lassen ihn so sehr avantgardistisch aussehen.

Classic items of furniture become timeless, meaning they can be placed in contemporary minimalist spaces with very attractive results.

Los muebles clásicos se vuelven atemporales y por ello fácilmente pueden ser colocados en espacios minimalistas contemporáneos con resultados muy atractivos.

Les meubles classiques sont intemporels, ils vont très bien dans des espaces minimalistes contemporains.

Die klassischen Möbel sind zeitlos und können daher leicht in moderne minimalistischen Räume integriert werden, was zu sehr attraktiven Ergebnissen führt.

Wood is the one material that never goes out of fashion: its use makes a space warmer or fresher, and also helps to maximize each of the storage areas, visually enriching the harmony of an interior space.

La madera es el material que nunca pasa de moda: su tratamiento puede hacer que un espacio sea más cálido o fresco y además permite maximizar cada uno de los espacios de guardado enriqueciendo visualmente la armonía de un espacio interior.

Le bois est un matériel qui ne vieillit pas, qui peut recréer un espace frais ou chaleureux et qui permet d'optimiser les espaces de rangement. Le bois enrichie et rétablit l'harmonie d'une pièce.

Holz ist das Material, was einfach nie aus der Mode kommt. Seine Behandlung kann einen Raum entweder wärmer oder kühler gestalten und außerdem maximiert es die Bereiche, die der Aufbewahrung dienen, und sorgt damit optisch für Harmonie.

large spaces

espacios amplios

grands espaces

weite räume

The gaze should light upon and contemplate each element placed in a space. Nothing should be left to chance in the arrangement, to ensure that this quality of beauty endures here in the perfection of the whole ambiance.

La mirada debe cruzar y contemplar cada elemento que se encuentra en el espacio. Nada debe ser dispuesto al azar para que esa cualidad sea permanente, la belleza reside aquí en el perfeccionamiento de toda la atmósfera.

Le regard doit se poser sur chacun des éléments d'une pièce. Rien ne doit être placé de manière aléatoire, c'est la condition sine qua non pour recréer une atmosphère aussi belle que parfaite.

Der Blick sollte jedes Element in dem Raum wahrnehmen können. Nichts sollte nach dem Zufallsprinzip angeordnet werden, damit diese Qualität dauerhaft erhalten bleibt. Die Schönheit liegt hier in der Perfektionierung der gesamten Atmosphäre.

Each piece has its given place, and the furniture draws attention to its design and function as much as the importance of comfort for the inhabitant.

Cada pieza posee un lugar privilegiado, el mobiliario exalta su diseño y función tanto como la importancia del confort para el habitante.

Chaque objet à sa place privilégiée. Le mobilier mettra en avant son design et sa fonction, qui sont aussi importants que le confort de l'habitant.

Jedes Stück hat einen privilegierten Platz, die Möbel heben ihr Design und ihre Funktion hervor, sowie die Bedeutung des Komforts für den Bewohner.

A double-height space is easy to adorn with hanging lampshades, chimneys or large windows. Colors may range from neutral to warm tones, depending on our personality.

Un espacio a doble altura fácilmente se puede engalanar con lámparas colgantes, chimeneas o amplios ventanales. Los colores pueden ir de neutros a cálidos acordes a nuestra personalidad.

Les luminaires suspendus, les cheminées et les verrières servent à embellir un espace avec double hauteur sous plafond. Nous pouvons choisir des couleurs neutres ou chaudes, pour refléter notre personnalité.

Eine doppelte Raumhöhe kann ganz einfach mit hängenden Lampen, Kaminen und großen Fenstern dekoriert werden. Die Farbpalette kann von neutral bis hin zu wärmeren Tönen verlaufen, je nach unserer Persönlichkeit.

FOTÓGRAFOS PHOTOGRAPHES FOTOGRAFEN

PHOTOGRAPHERS

Editado en Octubre de 2013. Impreso en China.

El cuidado de edición estuvo a cargo de

AM Editores S.A. de C.V.

Edited in October 2013. Printed in China.

Published by AM Editores S.A. de C.V.